The Art
of Simple

The Art of Simple

RECIPES AND IDEAS FOR
A CALMER WAY OF LIFE

Eleanor Ozich

PENGUIN BOOKS

– contents –

change

_____

Simplicity. Even the word itself seems to bring an immediate sense of calm. This word has taught me many wonderful things, but most of all, it's helped me to find the extraordinary beauty in the small, daily moments — the kind that might have easily been missed. These moments are essential for finding balance, clarity and a sense of contentment in a hurried world.

After the success of my first two books, *My Petite Kitchen Cookbook* and *My Family Table*, what followed was a whirlwind couple of years, working long, relentless hours, and losing sight of the everyday things that mattered to me the most. Even though I had a career that I loved, I felt as though I was being pulled in too many different directions, each day becoming more detached from the simple lifestyle that I desperately yearned to live.

It was time for a change, and so we moved from the hustle and bustle of the city to a little 1950s beach house nestled among native bush and beautiful birdsong in Titirangi, Auckland. It was here, in our little piece of the world, that I discovered a profound kind of happiness that had previously elluded me. The simplicity and beauty of it all slowly spread its magic through our home, encouraging us to shed the unnecessary layers and allowing us to find joy.

Life is full of tests and trials, and daily distractions can feel heavy. It's a story that is all too familiar for many of us: work deadlines, bills upon bills, health challenges, the struggles that can come with parenting. These challenges come with a myriad of emotions and can cause us to lose our centre, become unbalanced or feel overwhelmed.

Perhaps you feel the pressure to constantly strive for more? More money, more things, more success, more self-worth? I too had become fixated on chasing these things, in the hope that I would feel fulfilled. It's only now I'm beginning to understand that when you live with less, you end up with so much more.

Simple living isn't about determining how little we can live with; it's about celebrating the things we simply can't live without. And once you fall in love with the simple things, you'll wonder how you never noticed them before.

And so, next time you're outside, take a moment to appreciate the world around you — the contrasting shadows beneath your feet, the drifting clouds in the sky, the leaves rustling in the trees. Take the time to really savour a juicy, ripe plum or to admire the simple beauty of a passing butterfly.

This book encapsulates my family's simple approach to living, an approach that is by nature continually adapting and evolving, just like the seasons surrounding us. Admittedly, it was sometimes a struggle to balance writing with mothering three little ones. But I am thankful that the experience has helped me in the way I hope it will help you — reminding me with every story, idea and recipe to appreciate the simple things.

Love, Eleanor x

wake

———

The things you choose to do when you wake in the morning are not only an indicator of the quality of your day to come, but by extension, the quality of your life. Learning to enjoy a handful of simple morning rituals not only helps us to slow down, but to connect with the beautiful, everyday moments that we might otherwise miss.

Morning self-care is a beautiful way to fill your cup, and allows good feelings to overflow into the rest of your day. Taking the time to start the day well can also have a profound impact on the mindset we possess, the experiences we attract, and the energy we give out to others.

There's no particular formula for building your own ritual — the most important thing is that you find what works for you. Over the next few pages, I will share a few simple ideas that will help you begin your day with meaning and beauty.

Rise with the Sun

——————

Wake early with the sunrise, open your front door, and breathe in the fresh, cool air. Rising early not only helps us to connect to our body's natural rhythm, it can also satisfy the need for a peaceful and relaxing start to the day, particularly if you have children.

Once I'm out of bed, the first thing I do is make myself as comfortable as possible. If it's winter, I'll pop on a cashmere robe, put on some slippers and prepare that exquisite first cup of tea. In the summertime, I'll take a quick shower to wash away any remnants of drowsiness, then prepare a light and refreshing smoothie for breakfast.

If I have any creative writing to do, I often use these first few hours to work, as I'm at my most inspired first thing in the morning. Otherwise, I'll do some slow stretching, or go for a gentle walk. Whatever it is you like to do, choose your reason to get up early, and embrace the day with a head start.

Mango, Lime and Mint Smoothie

SERVES 2

½ cup fresh or frozen diced mango

1 frozen banana*

juice of ½ lime

1¼ cups coconut milk

2cm piece of fresh ginger

handful of fresh mint

handful of ice cubes

A light breakfast smoothie — bright, creamy and invigorating.

———————————

Put all the ingredients except a few of the mint leaves in a blender and blend until smooth. If necessary, add a little water or extra coconut milk to reach your desired consistency.

Pour into glasses, garnish with reserved mint leaves, and serve.

* You can use fresh banana if you don't have frozen, though frozen gives it a lovely thick consistency, like ice cream.

Carob, Fig and Vanilla Thickshake

SERVES 2

2 frozen bananas

300ml almond or coconut milk

1 heaped tbsp carob, plus a little for dusting

4 dried figs or dates

1 tsp pure vanilla extract

pinch of sea salt

I've had a real thing for carob lately, with its delicate malt flavour and soft, natural sweetness. In this morning shake, it's combined with frozen bananas, dried figs and a touch of pure vanilla for a heavenly start to the day.

_____

Put all the ingredients in a blender and blend until smooth.

Pour into glasses and dust with carob to serve.

Remind

———————

Write down your favourite quote, inspiring lyrics or meditative mantra. Tape it next to your wardrobe, or somewhere you will see it each morning. Each Sunday, replace it with a new quote to keep things fresh and inspiring. These words will be the first thing you see when you rise, and your final thoughts before sleep.

Awaken Your Senses

———————

Upon waking, splash your face with cold water a few times, and delight in its pure freshness. Not only does this help to awaken your senses, it also washes away the skin impurities and feeling of fogginess that can come with sleep. I also take this moment to drink a large glass of water with lemon or grapefruit, which helps me to rehydrate and kick-starts my digestion for the day.

Tahini and Maple Granola with Golden Berries

SERVES 10

3 tbsp tahini

4 tbsp maple syrup

2 tbsp coconut oil, melted

3 cups wholegrain oats

pinch of sea salt

½ cup dried inca berries*

½ cup dried blueberries*

Pure maple syrup is an interesting way to sweeten granola, and it combines beautifully with tahini, coconut oil and a flick of sea salt. If you don't have any maple syrup, honey is just as good. I've tossed the toasted granola with dried inca berries (commonly known in New Zealand as cape gooseberries) and blueberries for something a little bit fancy.

_____

Preheat the oven to 180°C.

Combine all the ingredients except for the dried berries in a large mixing bowl. Stir until combined, then spread the mixture out evenly on a tray lined with baking paper.

Roast for 12–15 minutes or until golden.

Leave to cool, then mix through the dried berries.

The granola will keep for up to 3 months if stored in a large glass jar or airtight container.

* You could use most types of dried fruit here.

Buttermilk Crêpes with Honey-poached Strawberries

SERVES 4

Poached strawberries

1½ cups fresh or frozen strawberries, hulled

¼ cup water

2 tbsp honey

Crêpes

1 cup spelt flour*

1 cup buttermilk**

4 free-range eggs

1 tsp vanilla

pinch of salt

To serve

natural or coconut yoghurt

In summer, there is often a punnet or two of fresh straw-berries in our kitchen. Cooked in a little water and honey, the fruit becomes sweet and sumptuous, and is delicious served on thin, delicate crêpes. The poached strawberries also make a lovely sauce to accompany yoghurt or vanilla ice cream.

―――――――――

Place the strawberries, water and honey in a small saucepan over medium heat and bring to a gentle boil. Lower heat and simmer for 15 minutes or until soft. Allow to cool, then transfer to a serving bowl and set aside. It will also keep for up to 5 days in a container in the fridge.

Put all the crêpe ingredients in the bowl of a food processor and blend until smooth.

Place a large skillet or pan over medium-low heat. Put some butter or coconut oil into the pan to melt and swirl around to evenly coat the base.

Add a third of a cup of the crêpe batter to the pan, swirling the pan to coat the base. Cook for 1–2 minutes on each side or until golden. Repeat with the remaining batter, keeping the stack of cooked crêpes warm in the oven if you like.

Serve the crêpes warm with natural or coconut yoghurt and poached strawberries on the side.

* Buckwheat, quinoa or rice flour can be used as a gluten-free alternative.

** Nut milk can be used as a dairy-free alternative.

Spiced Sweet Potato Pancakes

SERVES 4

100g orange sweet
potato, skin on, cubed

4 free-range eggs

½ cup rolled oats

¼ cup coconut, rapadura
or muscovado sugar

4 tbsp spelt or
buckwheat flour

1 tsp ground cinnamon

½ tsp ground nutmeg

pinch of ground
cardamom

2 tsp pure vanilla extract

pinch of sea salt

The homely scent of warm, sweet spices can arouse the senses like nothing else. During the colder months, these comforting sweet potato pancakes often make an appearance in our home, usually on a lazy Sunday morning.

———————

Place the sweet potato in a small saucepan, cover with water and bring to the boil. Simmer over a low heat for 10–15 minutes or until tender. Drain well, transfer to a blender and blend until puréed.

Add the remaining ingredients to the blender and blend until smooth.

Place a large skillet or pan over medium-low heat. Put some butter or coconut oil into the pan to melt and swirl around to evenly coat.

For each pancake, ladle 1 large tablespoon of batter into the pan; depending on the size of your pan you should be able to cook three pancakes at a time.

As soon as little bubbles start to appear, turn the pancakes over. Continue to cook for a further minute or so until dark golden brown. Repeat with remaining batter.

Serve the pancakes warm with your choice of toppings. We enjoy them with a drizzle of maple syrup and grilled bananas if we're feeling fancy.

Switch Off

Checking social media or scanning through emails first thing in the morning can become automatic. Not only does this hijack our focus and put us in a reactive state, it can often mean we put other's needs before our own. Next time you reach for your phone, do yourself a favour and turn off your notifications so you can embrace the morning with no distractions.

Morning Pages

You might have heard of this exercise, which involves putting pen to paper and writing about anything and everything on your mind, ideally first thing in the morning. I read about this technique in a book called *The Artist's Way* by Julia Cameron. There is no right or wrong way to do Morning Pages — you can write about whatever you like, whether it is something that is worrying you or an aspiration you have. This simple exercise can help you to clear your head, whether it's of small distracting thoughts, or more challenging issues. It's also a great way to gain focus and encourage clear and creative thinking.

Smile at Yourself in the Mirror

As silly as it sounds, this lovely ritual can boost your self-esteem and acts as a gentle reminder that you are in charge of your own happiness. You might be surprised at the positive thoughts it can inspire.

The Slowness of Tea

———

The simple task of preparing tea might just be my most treasured morning ritual of all. I like to treat the act of preparing tea as a way of practising mindfulness. Next time you pop the kettle on, relish each step of the process, sip slowly, and take the time to appreciate the delicious aroma. I enjoy rooibos tea with its soft, caramel flavour; it's lovely with a little honey and a splash of almond milk.

Butter Tea

SERVES 1

1 cup freshly brewed
black or rooibos tea

2 tbsp good-quality
unsalted butter,
or 1 tbsp butter and
1 tbsp coconut oil

Optional additions

½ tsp pure vanilla extract

pinch of cinnamon

1 tsp honey

Butter tea is a traditional beverage from Tibet, where
the nourishing benefits of butter are said to provide
much-needed sustenance in the bitterly cold mountains.
Locals drink this creamy tea throughout the day to
maintain energy and nourish the mind, body and spirit.
I like to start my day with a small, light breakfast, but
sometimes a warm mug of butter tea hits the spot, while
providing a boost of healthy fats. Butter tea kick-starts
the metabolism, provides a sustained sense of energy
throughout the day, and is even said to boost brain power.
The butter lends a surprisingly creamy, silky texture,
similar to a latte.

Put all the ingredients in a blender and blend until creamy.

Enjoy immediately.

simplify

How we keep our home is essentially how we choose to live. I imagine the home to be a celebration of the everyday, a place that strikes the perfect balance between beautiful and practical, with each being an expression of who we are.

It's wonderful to own things you love, but by acquiring them sparingly the appreciation is so much more satisfying.

Over the past ten years we have moved a number of times, and with each move it felt natural to let go of things that added clutter to our home. I realised I only needed to keep and acquire things that I found very beautiful, that bring immense joy, or that are useful on a daily basis.

Not only did I find I was able to live without a lot of things, I began to feel much happier, more fulfilled, and had a sense of calm that only simplicity can bring.

Whether items in your home are broken, carry bad memories, or serve no practical purpose, we can benefit in so many ways from simplifying and learning to let go of the things that no longer serve us. In this chapter, I share some ideas to help inspire you to live with less, and in turn, find joy in so much more.

Where to Start?

———————

The idea of decluttering might seem daunting, and perhaps you're asking yourself where to start. There's no particular strategy for simplifying, although however you do it, it's important to take your first step with excitement behind it. There's a world of freedom behind the clutter, you simply have to start.

First things first, ensure you are in a relaxed, happy mood, and have an hour or so to spare. I find it helpful to work on one small area at a time, usually in the early afternoon when my youngest is asleep. If you try to do the whole house at once it will be far too overwhelming, and you might be easily defeated or frustrated. Put some inspiring and positive music on in the background, and choose a room or area to begin with.

Start by having a rubbish bag ready, and a box for the items you wish to sell or give away to a local charity store.

Pick up each item and consider whether it gets used often, whether it makes your heart sing, or brings warm, happy memories. Be ruthlessly honest with yourself. If the item isn't useful, beautiful or meaningful, it's time to be free of its clutter — let it go.

You might find you know exactly what you want to keep and which things belong in the rubbish or at the charity store. But then there are the items you don't use but think you might want, or need, someday. You might like to create a 'maybe' box filled with these particular items. Store the box somewhere out of the way. Pull it out six months later and see if there's anything you really needed. Usually, you can just donate the whole box, because you never really needed those items anyway.

Once you've finished decluttering that area, ensure you finish the job. Take the rubbish out to the bin, or drive to the local charity shop and donate the items. It's too easy to put this off until later, when you might be tempted to return items to the house.

Now that you've completed that area, take a moment to enjoy its beautiful simplicity. It's a lovely look, don't you think?

Simple Habits for an Uncluttered Home

Consider your home when it feels cosy and inviting. It's likely to be much more relaxing and aesthetically appealing when it's at its tidiest — better still, when it's clean, unfussy and thoughtfully decorated.

It takes just a little bit longer to put things away in an orderly fashion than it does to do it in a disorderly way, but the result is disproportionately better. In fact, the virtue of tidiness can be introduced to all areas of your home, so long as you change your perspective on the matter. Try to imagine the process as an expression of how much you appreciate your home, rather than it being a chore that you despise.

Find the areas in your home that accumulate clutter, and undertake to keep them clear. These are likely to be the high-traffic areas of your home, such as the entrance, dining room table or kitchen bench. Keeping these areas clear can be as simple as having a designated place for your belongings. Allocate a series of hooks for keys, a shelf in the cupboard for your handbag, a desk for your children's homework and a tray or filing system for the miscellaneous letters and paper that always seem to cause disarray. It might take a few extra seconds to put everything in its proper place, but you'll be glad you did so.

Hidden-away areas such as cupboards, drawers and underneath the bed can easily attract clutter. Despite being out of sight, the build-up of things in these areas can affect us just as much as the clutter in the visible areas does — just knowing it's there can make you feel overwhelmed and frustrated. Aim to organise one area a day, or one a week. Most of the time, you'll find that the things that have been hidden away are no longer useful or appreciated.

Take note of the things you bring into your home. Each time you want to buy something that's not absolutely necessary, give yourself a week or two to think about it first. More often than not, the need (or want) for a particular item wavers, or we forget about it altogether. If you do end up buying something new, make a rule that for every new item that comes into your life, you must let go of one in return.

Once tidying and simplifying has become an everyday habit and you recognise it as a means to a beautiful, inspired style of living, you might begin to enjoy it.

Fall in Love with Your Home

———————

Our homes and the rooms they hold mean different things to each of us. For some, an inviting space for entertaining might be the most loved space in the home, for others a cosy and relaxed bedroom might be the perfect place for a little sanctuary.

Simple, beautiful decorating isn't about perfect arrangements or spending copious amounts on the latest trend, it's about finding joy in the small pleasures. Whatever your personality or style might be, it's entirely up to you to create an aesthetically pleasing environment to live in.

Ideas to Refresh Your Home

———

No matter how seemingly 'finished' your décor might be, an inspiring sense of change in your home is always welcome, and the more you enjoy your space, the more you'll take care of it — and vice versa. Instead of allowing mess to accumulate on your kitchen bench, you'll begin to feel inspired to declutter and perhaps create a pleasing arrangement in its place. Or instead of letting piles of laundry build up in the corner of the living room, you'll fold it nicely and put it away.

Whether you live in a house that you own or a small, rented apartment, here are some simple and low-cost ideas that will instantly refresh your home.

The simple act of cleaning windows and mirrors can create a brighter, sparklier home. While you're at it, wipe down any light fixtures, lamps and tabletops. These areas can accumulate quite a bit of dust and grime, making a noticeable difference when cleaned.

A natural woven basket or two can bring texture to your home, as will pillows and throws. I like to soften each room by introducing fabrics and items that have texture, creating cosiness and warmth.

Sometimes all a room needs is a pop of colour. If your home seems a little dull, or it feels like something is missing, a floral arrangement or a few sprigs of foliage should do the trick. This could be a single large leaf in a vase or a few stems of lovely flowers. Nature provides one of the easiest ways to bring your space to life.

Introduce a houseplant or two. Not only are indoor plants beautiful and mood enhancing, they are also nature's way of helping to refresh the air, constantly working to convert carbon dioxide into oxygen. Some plants can even remove toxins from your home, improving air quality. If you already care for a few, perhaps try moving them around to refresh your space.

Make the most of the sunshine and launder your soft furnishings. This simple process can give your whole place a lift, creating a fresh and clean feeling. Leave your pillow covers, curtains and smaller rugs to dry outside — the sun will naturally whiten them. Once you've pinned them on the line, take a moment to appreciate your handy work and enjoy a sparkling lemonade on the deck while they dry in the warm breeze.

Move
Twenty-seven
Things

———————

There's a simple yet surprisingly effective feng shui method that can help to create positive energy and an inspiring sense of change in your home. All you have to do is 'move' twenty-seven things. For example, you could beautify a shelf by placing on it a few things you'd like to admire each day, you might clear some clutter and donate items to those in need, or perhaps change your pillow cases, and then drape a thick, luscious blanket over the end of your bed. It's the little, thoughtful changes that cultivate a sense of harmony and calm around you. You might even notice a new love and appreciation for the things you own — I certainly do.

Indoor Greenery

———

In the same way that I would choose a piece of furniture, I choose indoor greenery with much care and consideration. As well as improving air quality and mood, thoughtfully placed plants are the perfect way to add vibrancy, texture and colour to a space.

Empty gaps beside chairs or other furniture are a great spot for oversized plants, or a tall leafy palm in the corner of a room is another thought. If you have limited room terrariums are a space-saving way to incorporate some greenery, and a few pots of herbs on your kitchen windowsill can add a burst of colour and fragrance.

Beautify Your Shelves

———————

Bookshelves are not confined to holding literature, they can also be an opportunity to make a beautiful statement in the room.

Begin by placing a selection of your most-loved books, some vertically and some horizontally. I like to pepper the colours around evenly for a collected, yet balanced, look.

Mix it up by adding objects of interest — things you've collected from far-flung places, or that lovely ornament you picked up from the thrift store. Include various textures, sizes and colours.

Next, add something organic. This could be an interesting shell, a small cactus plant or a honey-coloured candle.

Then take a few steps back to consider your shelves. Is there balance within the imperfection? Is it pleasing to the eye? If there's a large stack of books on one side, you might like to balance it out with a large ornament or plant on the other.

Last but not least, ensure you change it up often. It's such a simple way to keep things new and inspiring.

A Minimalist Bedroom

Our bedroom is too small to house more furniture than the bed and two round wicker stools that we use as bedside tables. There's a small sliding wardrobe for our clothes (mostly on hangers) and a few shelves for footwear.

When we first moved in, I was worried about where everything would go, but in hindsight, the tiny room has been a blessing in disguise. It inspired us to create a light, airy and uncluttered space, perfect in its simplicity. It's the room in which I feel the most relaxed and calm, and I believe it's because it has so little in it.

A Clear, Bright Bathroom

It doesn't always take a major renovation to turn your bathroom into a happy space — sometimes a few small changes can make all the difference. It might have finishes that wouldn't have been your first choice, and sometimes these can easily be replaced to create a whole new look. Here are a few ideas for creating a clear, bright bathroom, without spending a ton.

Luscious greenery is a lovely touch, particularly when paired with simple white walls. I also love a woven basket or two for laundry, toilet rolls or any other loose items that need to be stored.

If there are countless bottles of products and toiletries on your sink top and many more hidden away underneath, it's time to have a sort through and keep only those you use regularly. Store them neatly in the drawer below, saving the counter space for your prettiest items.

Create a little luxury every day by arranging a stack of beautiful, luscious towels and a few thoughtfully placed candles on a shelf. It's the little touches that can make your bathroom feel fresh and interesting.

The Simple Kitchen

When I imagine the perfect home-cooking space, I envision a basic, uncluttered kitchen, one with only the essentials; there's nothing more satisfying than coming home to a clean, organised kitchen with each pot, cookbook and serving bowl neatly in its place.

Much like the same decluttering process I talked about earlier, it's important to regularly sort through the items in your kitchen and let go of those you don't need. This applies to your drawers, cupboards, and last but not least, your fridge and freezer. You might even discover a new sense of energy and motivation to spend time in the kitchen, even after a modest bout of decluttering.

Here are a few ideas for keeping your kitchen both beautiful *and* practical.

We all have our own idea of what is necessary in the kitchen — it is, after all, a uniquely personal space. Personally, I prefer glass storage containers over plastic; not only are they prettier, and a healthier way to store food, but they last much longer, too. The same applies for wooden utensils, which I've never had to throw out — I can't say the same about plastic versions.

Cotton storage bags are an earth-friendly companion to take along with you to the local farmers' market or grocery store. The best part is that you can use them over and over again, and pop them in the washing machine if need be. Linen dish covers can be used in place of cling-film. Beeswax food wrap is another idea to keep your food fresh without plastic; simply use the warmth of your hands to mould the beeswax around the top of a bowl or serving dish.

The day before we go food shopping, I like to evaluate the contents of our fridge, freezer and pantry. Are there perishables past their prime? How long has that jar of pickles been lurking in the back of the fridge? What's that unrecognisable container of something in the freezer that's just begging to be thrown away? When in doubt, throw it out — it's as simple as that.

One of the easiest ways to keep your kitchen looking clutter-free is to keep the counter space as clear as possible. Once you have tucked everything neatly away, select a handful of pieces you're especially fond of and put them on display. This could be a cast-iron skillet you use daily, a ceramic jar filled with beautiful utensils, or a small arrangement of elegantly worn cutting boards. These little touches will add character to your kitchen, yet still lend a minimalist look.

leafy greens
lemons
raspberries
two dozen eggs
Sourdough
butter beans
lentils
natural yoghurt
Parmesan
unsalted butter
coconut oil

Simplify Your Shopping List

———

In my kitchen, simplicity is most definitely the greatest virtue. It goes without saying that the same applies to my shopping list each week. Here's a breakdown of our typical shopping list, and a few ideas on the matter.

———

Plenty of seasonal fruit and vegetables. We eat a largely plant-based diet so quality produce is essential to inspire simple meals. I usually shop at the farmers' market or the local grocer. There are always plenty of leafy greens for salads, summery stews, soups and smoothies, and I often freeze any leftover dark greens to avoid waste. Bananas are a staple in our house, simply eaten as they are, as a topping on oatmeal, in smoothies or in banana bread. When it comes to fresh produce let the seasons guide you and buy local if possible.

Lots of legumes, such as lentils, butter beans and chickpeas. The perfect base for a simple nutritious meal — imagine a herby lentil salad with mustard vinaigrette, chickpeas braised in a rich tomato sauce and served with crusty sourdough bread, buttered balsamic lentils, or perhaps a garlicky butter-bean hummus (see recipe on page 156).

Free-range, organic eggs. The humble egg makes a nutritious breakfast, lunch or dinner. It's not surprising that our family get through two dozen a week. They're also an essential ingredient in most of our homemade baking. Eggs are a necessity to have on hand for hungry little tummies.

A loaf or two of sourdough bread. We just love its complex, chewy quality and delicious hint of sourness, a character that comes from fermentation of the dough. We also find it's much easier to digest compared to commercially made bread.

Good-quality dairy. I usually buy a wedge of Parmesan or Pecorino, a block of sheep's feta, and some nice Cheddar for the kids. There'll be a block or two of nice butter, and a small bottle of organic cream as I like a dash in my morning coffee. If I feel like splashing out, I'll get a jar of coconut yoghurt, although a thick natural yoghurt is also nice. If you prefer to be dairy-free, there's a plethora of coconut and nut alternatives out there, or you could try to make your own as this tends to be much more cost-effective.

Rolled oats. This humble and low-cost ingredient is not only essential for our morning oatmeal (always soaked overnight for easier digestion), I often use it in baking instead of flour or ground nuts. Simply grind the oats in your food processor until you have a flour-like consistency.

Store-cupboard staples. These items are key to keeping the price of your weekly shop down, and I stock up on them once every couple of months, or as needed. My shopping list includes rice, quinoa, polenta, pasta, olives, sundried tomatoes, capers, plus dried goods for baking, such as buckwheat flour, spelt flour, dried coconut, various seeds and nuts, baking soda, and rapadura or coconut sugar. A large bottle of extra virgin olive oil for drizzling and a jar of coconut oil for cooking. Apple cider vinegar for health tonics and dressings, some good-quality honey, and dried herbs, spices and stock — always important for flavouring meals.

Fish. We enjoy fish once or twice a week, but only occasionally buy meat these days. There are a few reasons for this choice: the effect on the environment being one, and we have also found a new sense of energy and health from eating a more plant-based diet. When I do eat meat, I appreciate it more than I used to. If you do eat meat regularly the butcher is a great place to buy it, particularly for cheaper cuts, or if you have access to it, home-kill meat is another great idea that is cost-effective.

Simple One-pot Pasta

SERVES 4

glug of extra virgin
olive oil

6 shallots, roughly
chopped

bunch of asparagus,
woody ends removed
and discarded, sliced
at an angle

250g dried pasta*

large handful of fresh
oregano, roughly
chopped

2 large handfuls of fresh
basil, roughly chopped

juice of 1 large lemon

2 tbsp butter

I've seen quite a few variations of one-pot pasta floating around. If you haven't tried this no-fuss technique, I gently urge you to do so — it's simply too easy not to try. I've used delicate-stemmed asparagus, as it's a lovely way to savour this vegetable during its short season. The dried pasta is cooked with the other ingredients and the starch creates a meltingly delicious sauce. It's probably one of the easiest dinners I've ever made and the variations are endless, too.

Add enough olive oil to a heavy-bottomed cast-iron pot to cover the bottom. Heat the oil gently over medium heat.

Add the shallots and asparagus and stir to coat in the oil. Sauté gently for 2–3 minutes, stirring continuously.

Add the pasta and enough boiling water to just cover it. Bring back to a soft boil then lower the heat and simmer, stirring occasionally, until the pasta is al dente. The liquid should have reduced, creating a light, starchy sauce.

Add the herbs, lemon juice and butter. Season generously with flaky sea salt and freshly ground pepper, then toss until the pasta is evenly coated in the sauce.

Serve immediately with a drizzle of extra virgin olive oil and an extra squeeze of lemon if you desire.

* I used gluten-free sorghum pasta, although most types
   of dried pasta are fine, simply adjust the cooking times
   accordingly. If the pasta looks dry while cooking, just add a
   little more water to the pot.

cleanse

————

Learning to enjoy the ritual of cleaning can bring a sense of calm and loveliness to your daily chores. In this chapter you'll find a collection of simple, natural cleaning recipes for beauty, laundry and home. From the ingredients used to the pretty glass jars they are stored in, I believe home-made formulations can bring immense joy and a sense of satisfaction.

A Skincare Routine

———

We can all benefit from embracing a beauty routine, even a very simple one. I prefer to use a basic selection of natural products on my skin, such as coconut oil, witch hazel and rose water. This extends to the products I use on my children.

I find having a simple yet thoughtful skincare ritual far more enjoyable than one encumbered by many ingredient-dense products, and it's particularly enhanced by using products that are lovingly homemade. I find my complexion is more radiant, silky and smooth. There are some fantastic natural cosmetics being made, and I use just a light all-natural foundation during the day. A natural sunscreen is also a good idea.

The thing with natural cosmetics is that they have a much shorter shelf life than their commercial counterparts, so I usually only make small amounts. It's about being intentional with what you use, shopping differently, and buying far less.

Here are some simple skincare recipes that take only moments to prepare, and don't cost the earth.

Witch Hazel Toner

MAKES 100ML

Coconut Oil Cleanser

Gently massage a small amount of coconut oil into your skin in a circular motion. Using a warm, damp facecloth, remove any residue and makeup. If you have sensitive or oily skin, you might like to dilute the coconut oil in warm water. Store it in a dark-coloured glass jar.

Witch hazel is a natural extract derived from the bark and leaves of the shrub of that name, and has a long history of use, particularly in natural medicine and skincare. This natural astringent is gentle to use, and is excellent for helping to reduce the appearance of acne, redness and irritation. It also helps to lock in moisture and balance oily or dry skin types. I've also included rose water in this recipe, as it's said to help prevent signs of ageing and keep your skin feeling rejuvenated and beautifully soft.

50ml witch hazel extract
50ml rose water

Pour the witch hazel and rose water into a small spray bottle and shake gently to combine.

Spray onto the skin after cleansing. Allow to dry before applying moisturiser or face oil.

Brown Sugar Body Scrub

MAKES ABOUT 2 CUPS

1 cup golden sugar
(I used muscovado but
coconut sugar also
works well)

1 cup almond oil or
melted coconut oil

a few drops of essential
oil of your choice
(optional)

I always feel lovely and refreshed after a good exfoliating scrub. This simple scrub smells delicious and can be used just on your face or your whole body.

Combine all the ingredients and store in a dark-coloured airtight jar.

I like to use this scrub about once a week. To use, gently exfoliate skin with 1–2 tablespoons of the scrub and rinse with warm water.

Apple Cider and Honey Shampoo

MAKES ABOUT 375ML

¼ cup raw honey

¼ cup apple cider
vinegar

1 cup filtered water

This gentle, nourishing and all-natural hair rinse is made
from just three ingredients — raw honey, apple cider
vinegar and filtered water. Honey doesn't strip the hair
of natural oils and leaves your hair feeling incredibly
soft, silky and shiny. Be aware that it does not lather
like store-bought shampoo, and can take a little getting
used to! After using it for a month or so you might notice
that you can go longer between washes and no longer
need conditioner, as it normalises the oil production in
your hair.

Put all the ingredients into a glass bottle (I like to use an
empty apple cider vinegar bottle). Shake well to dissolve
the honey and combine.

To use, wet your hair as usual and pour about a quarter of
a cup through your hair. Massage gently and then rinse.

Eucalyptus and Lime Liquid Hand Soap

MAKES ABOUT 500ML

300ml filtered water

a bar of Castile soap, finely grated

10 drops of eucalyptus essential oil

10 drops of lime essential oil

3 tbsp sweet almond oil

I often find commercially made hand soap leaves my skin feeling dry, and so I created a homemade version that's much gentler. I've paired eucalyptus and lime for an invigorating fresh aroma, and a dash of almond oil to soften the skin. I use two 250ml bottles with pump nozzles so that I can pop one into each bathroom.

Put the water and grated soap in a small saucepan over low heat. Stir continuously until the soap dissolves.

Allow to cool.

Stir in the oils then pour into dark-coloured bottles.

Homemade Baby Wipes

MAKES 100ML

80ml filtered water

20ml witch hazel extract

a few drops chamomile
or calendula essential oil
(optional)

Not only are disposable wipes expensive and awful for the environment, but they tend to contain fragrances, preservatives and chemicals that can be harsh on babies' skin. I like to keep it simple and make my own baby wipe solution using witch hazel extract and filtered water. Witch hazel is soothing, antibacterial and has a wonderfully clean fragrance. A few drops of chamomile or calendula essential oil can be added for sensitive skin.

Pour ingredients into a glass container (use dark-coloured glass if using essential oils) and shake gently to combine. Place reusable muslin or cotton wipes in the solution to soak and use as needed.

You could also store the solution in a small spray bottle and spray onto the wipes prior to use. I find this easier for when I'm out and about.

Natural Insect Repellent

MAKES 100ML

50ml filtered water

50ml witch hazel

Your choice of:
 citronella
 peppermint
 eucalyptus
 lemongrass
 tea tree
 peppermint
 lavender
 rose geranium
 bergamot
 lemon

This insect repellent only takes minutes to make, and smells wonderful. I always have a bottle on hand for summer evening barbecues, or picnics at the beach. Store-bought repellents can often contain nasty chemicals, so I love that this homemade version uses all-natural ingredients and is nice and gentle on the skin. I've included a list of essential oils that are effective bug deterrents. I like a combination of lavender and bergamot, but you can try different variations to suit your preference.

In a small spray bottle, combine water and witch hazel, and then add 15–20 drops of the essential oils of your choice.

Shake gently to combine before using.

A Beautiful
Laundry Routine

———

With pretty, useful tools and a few simple ideas, you might feel inspired to create your own enjoyable laundry routine.

———

Invest in a lovely looking laundry basket. Whatever your aesthetic might be, vintage-look wire or natural and woven, it makes for a pleasant place for your clothes to hang out until you are ready to fold them.

If you're washing items like lingerie, soft knit sweaters, or other delicate clothing, separate them from the rest of your load, and place them into a mesh bag before placing them into the machine. It will keep them in good shape and make them last a lot longer. This is a simple habit to get into, but one many people forget.

Wool dryer balls are now fairly easy to find and they help to keep your laundry soft, knock out wrinkles and reduce the drying time. They are completely natural, being made from felted wool, and seem to last forever. Simply pop them in your dryer along with your clean washing. Your wallet (and the planet) will thank you!

If you have a large family, get into the habit of doing a load of washing each day. When it comes to folding it and putting it away, it won't take you as long as a week's worth will and won't feel like such a chore. Just make sure that if it is not a full load, you set the water level to medium or low so as not to use more water than needed.

Next time you fold the washing, play some relaxing music — or enjoy silence if that's your thing — and take your time, intentionally turning the chore into a joyous moment.

Putting clothes away is much more pleasant when you don't have to stuff them into already-crammed drawers or cluttered shelves. Friends are often surprised when they see how sparse my wardrobe is, which usually consists of only 10–15 items of clothing. I'm content wearing the same, beautiful clothes in heavy rotation — in fact it makes life so much easier! Each item is considered carefully for its practicality, quality and ability to mix and match. It's also a great exercise in finding your true style.

Washing Powder

MAKES 2 CUPS

You can add a few drops of essential oil to this washing powder if you would like to add a little fragrance. Citrus oils work well, such as lemon, lime or grapefruit. Lavender is always nice, too. I recommend wearing gloves when handling borax, as it can sometimes irritate sensitive skin.

———————

a bar of unscented natural soap, grated (such as beeswax or goat's milk)

¾ cup borax

½ cup baking soda

20 drops of essential oil of your choice (optional, I like lemon, lime and grapefruit)

Put all the ingredients into the bowl of a food processor and process until a fine powder.

Use 2–3 tablespoons per load of washing.*

* I always wash using cold water, but if you find that your washing powder does not dissolve properly in cold, you can dissolve it in hot water before adding it to the washing machine, or do a warm-water wash.

Fabric Softener

Add ⅔ cup white vinegar to the beginning of your wash cycle, along with your washing powder, to soften clothes and keep colours lovely and vibrant.

Odour Remover

Add ¾ cup baking soda to the beginning of your wash cycle, along with your washing powder, to remove particularly strong odours.

Vanilla and Rose Linen Water

MAKES ABOUT 100ML

20ml rose water

80ml distilled water

5 drops rose essential oil

10 drops vanilla
essential oil

Mist your fabrics with delicately scented linen water for a pleasurable ironing experience. The pure scent of this vanilla and rose blend will instantly refresh your clothing and homewares. Linen water makes a lovely gift; include a handwritten label for a pretty finishing touch.

———————————

Put all the ingredients in a small, dark-coloured spray bottle.

Shake gently to combine and use as needed.

Earth-friendly Cleaning

———

Keeping a clean and tidy home helps me to feel clear-minded, inspired and grounded. Since clearing the clutter and learning to live with fewer things, I've found it far easier to keep on top of it all, too. Rather than putting off cleaning for days at a time, then having to tackle one big mess later down the track, I've incorporated it into our daily rhythms, and it works a charm.

I love making my own natural and earth-friendly cleaning supplies, made out of simple, low-cost ingredients. Over the next few pages, I've gathered a few simple recipes that you might like to try out at home. Feel free to play around with your own essential oils, creating beautiful and unique aromas.

Grapefruit and Lime All-purpose Spray

MAKES ABOUT 500ML

2 tsp baking soda

2 tsp liquid castile soap

10 drops grapefruit essential oil

10 drops lime essential oil

475ml hot water

I make up a bottle of this all-purpose spray every other week, as I use it on almost everything! The pure essential oils in this formula not only smell delicious, they're also antibacterial and clean surfaces beautifully.

Put all the ingredients into a dark-coloured spray bottle and shake to combine before each use.

Citrus Air Freshener

MAKES ABOUT 100ML

10 drops lemon essential oil

5 drops sweet orange or lime essential oil

90ml filtered water

This citrus spray is great for purifying the air, and particularly for any lingering odours in the kitchen. During the colder months, I'll switch out the citrus oil for something a little more aromatic, such as bergamot, vetiver or pine. Lavender is always lovely, too.

Put all the ingredients into a dark-coloured spray bottle. Shake gently to combine.

Store in a cool, dark place, and use as needed.

Sweet Orange and Lemon Window Cleaner

MAKES ABOUT 500ML

400ml water (distilled or filtered is best so it doesn't leave a residue)

70ml white vinegar

10 drops sweet orange essential oil

10 drops lemon essential oil

2 tbsp liquid castile soap

I find myself wiping sticky fingerprints off the windows most days, and this sweet and citrusy cleaner does the job rather nicely. I've tried a few different ratios with the ingredients, and this version leaves the windows looking sparkly and clean.

Pour all the ingredients into a dark-coloured spray bottle.

To use, shake gently to combine and spray directly onto windows or glass surfaces.

Wipe clean using a microfibre cloth.

Toilet Cleaner

MAKES 1 CUP

½ cup baking soda

½ cup white vinegar

Because baking soda and vinegar get a little excited when mixed together, you'll need to make this cleaner as needed.

Pour the baking soda in and around the toilet bowl and then add the white vinegar.

Allow to fizz and leave it to do its magic for a few minutes or so.

Scrub well, and then flush.

Paste Cleaner

MAKES ABOUT ½ CUP

¼ cup borax

¼ cup baking soda

3–5 tbsp liquid castile soap

5 drops tea tree oil

This paste cleaner can be useful to combat mould and mildew and can also be used as an oven cleaner. I recommend wearing gloves when handling borax, as it can sometimes irritate sensitive skin.

Place the borax and baking soda in a bowl and pour in the liquid soap a little at a time, stirring gently until the consistency is creamy and smooth. Add the tea tree oil and stir to combine.

To use, dip a sponge or cloth into the mixture, scrub the surface, and rinse with water.

Black Tea Rust Cleaner

MAKES 800ML

2–3 black tea bags

800ml boiling water

I've used this simple remedy for cleaning jar lids and utensils, as well as garden tools.

Brew a pot of black tea using 2–3 tea bags and the boiling water.

Remove rust on small items by soaking them in the tea and then wiping away the rust.

Basic Wood Cleaner

MAKES ABOUT 250ML

125ml lemon juice
75ml filtered water
1 tsp liquid castile soap
3 tbsp olive oil

A simple recipe to nourish and restore wooden chopping boards, furniture or shelves. This cleaner must be used within two days, as the fresh lemon juice doesn't keep for long.

Put the ingredients in a bowl and stir to combine.

Dip a cloth into the solution and squeeze out any excess.

Wipe over surfaces, cleaning away dust, dirt or grime.

Almond Oil
Floor Polish

MAKES 500ML

125ml almond oil
250ml filtered water
125ml white vinegar

This polish couldn't be simpler to make, and adds a lovely shine to wooden floors. If you don't have any almond oil, olive oil also works well.

Pour ingredients into a spray bottle and shake until well combined.

Spray onto the bottom of a dust mop before using.

Tea Tree Spray for Mould

MAKES 100ML

15 drops tea tree oil

100ml filtered water

Tea tree oil has wonderful anti-fungal properties, and will naturally clean mould and mildew. It also helps to kill the spores and prevent future growth from happening. I use this spray every couple of weeks, and more so in the colder months, when dampness tends to linger.

———————————

Pour the ingredients into a dark-coloured spray bottle and shake to combine before each use.

Spray in the shower, bath or on the walls — wherever mould or mildew might be — leave for a few hours, and then wipe away.

cherish

The ebb and flow of our daily lives can sometimes seem mundane, and more often than not we become too busy or distracted to appreciate the small, beautiful moments that knit it all together. We are generally good at taking notice of the bigger things — the milestones, accomplishments, and achievements we experience — but what would happen if we gave ourselves permission to celebrate the little things, too?

These little things, these seemingly simple moments, can fill you up slowly but surely and help you to live a full and satisfying life. It's about engaging in meaningful moments, such as spending time with those you love, turning your everyday chores into pleasurable experiences, and cherishing the tiny happenings that would otherwise go unnoticed.

Take a
Daydream Break

When was the last time you daydreamed, allowing your mind to spontaneously wander wherever it might like to go?

There were many times in the past where instead of allowing this to happen I would reach for my phone, filling my mind with distractions as I scrolled through photos of other people's lives, or needlessly refreshed my email for the twentieth time that day. Rather than observing the beautiful world around me and allowing my thoughts to unwind, I'd be busily checking off my mental to-do list and adding cluttered thoughts to my mind.

Allowing yourself to daydream gives your mind a much-needed break, and it's a wonderful way to spark ideas and creativity. How many times have you had an epiphany while doing mindless chores, or broken through a mental block while going for a run? Our ability to drift off into space is surprisingly easy, and once you start, you might feel inspired to take a daydream break more often.

The Rhythm
of Cooking

———————

There's a beauty in the rhythm of cooking, a melody that can only be heard when preparing a meal peacefully. The gentle drum of a knife, slicing a beetroot on an old wooden board, hot oil sizzling and shimmering with fragrant herbs, onion and a little garlic. Perhaps it's the gentle bubbling of salted water, simmering softly in a large, heavy pot. These simple, beautiful moments can easily be lost, but are certainly not ordinary.

Next time you cook a meal, embrace slowness and focus on each step, allowing your mind to soften and your senses to be ignited. If you usually see cooking as a mundane chore you might find that you begin to see it as a pleasure, and a way to sow love into a nourishing meal for yourself, your family and friends.

The Family Meal

During the warmer months we often enjoy dinner out-doors. It's such a lovely way to eat, and mess doesn't matter quite so much. We head up the garden path and gather around a weathered old table, a selection of fragrant dishes and plenty of seasonal vegetables on offer. The cicadas sing happily in the background, accompanied by the gentle rustle of nature. Stories are shared while plates are passed around, filling our bellies and warming our cheeks.

Since having my own children, I've come to appreciate how special this ritual can be. The family meal is often where the deepest and most beautiful memories are formed; it's a chance to touch base and spend quality time together, no matter the menu or the weather.

Red Peppers with Rosemary and Chorizo

SERVES 4

2 tbsp olive oil

4 chorizo sausages, sliced into rounds

6 cloves garlic, finely chopped

2 tbsp fresh rosemary, finely sliced

1 tbsp smoked paprika

2 large peppers, sliced into strips (I used red and yellow)

4 courgettes, sliced into rounds

5 large tomatoes, roughly chopped, or 1 can chopped tomatoes

200ml red wine

2 cups chicken or vegetable stock

A sumptuous, fragrant stew of peppers, red wine and garlic. I've included chorizo for its rich, vibrant warmth, although it's just as good without if you are vegetarian.

Heat the oil in a casserole or large pan over medium heat. Cook the chorizo on each side until lightly golden, about 2–3 minutes. Transfer the chorizo to a plate, and set aside.

Add the garlic, rosemary and smoked paprika to the casserole, and sauté until fragrant, being careful not to brown. Add the peppers and courgettes, and cook, stirring every so often, for about 5 minutes. Add the chorizo, tomatoes, red wine and stock, bring to a simmer and turn the heat down to low.

Cook for 20–25 minutes, or until most of the liquid has cooked off. Season with sea salt and freshly ground pepper.

Serve warm with pasta, rice or some good bread. A sprinkling of Parmesan is nice, too.

Celebrate Sweet Food

———

There is so much pleasure to be had in enjoying a little something sweet every now and then, and I believe there is no reason why you shouldn't enjoy the sweet foods that you love. The key is to really savour them.

Next time you enjoy a sweet delight, pay close attention to each and every flavour you taste. It's a wonderful way to eat mindfully and enjoy food in all its beauty, whether it's the bittersweet of chocolate, the tanginess of lemon curd, or the crispy crust of perfectly golden pastry.

But most of all, as you relish each and every mouthful, indulge in knowing that you deserve it.

Dark Chocolate, Prune and Hazelnut Torte

MAKES ONE 23CM CAKE

300g good-quality dark chocolate, melted

1 cup unsalted butter or coconut oil

¾ cup coconut, rapadura or muscovado sugar

½ cup hazelnut meal*

1 cup prunes

2 tsp pure vanilla extract

6 free-range eggs

pinch of sea salt

To serve

icing sugar

fresh fruit

It's hard not to love a decadent, moist chocolate cake. This recipe is not overly sweet, and has a soft, sensuous texture from the prunes. Serve with cream or vanilla ice cream, in appropriately small slices.

Preheat the oven to 170°C and grease a 23cm cake tin with butter or coconut oil.

Put all the ingredients into the bowl of a food processor and blend until smooth.

Tip the mixture into the prepared cake tin and use a spatula to smooth out evenly.

Bake for 20–25 minutes or until a skewer inserted in the middle comes out clean. It can burn easily, so be sure to keep an eye on it.

Remove from the oven and leave to cool in the tin.

Once cooled, carefully remove from the tin. If serving immediately, dust with icing sugar and garnish with fresh fruit of your choice.

Will keep in an airtight container for up to 5 days.

* You could use any type of ground nuts here, such as almonds or walnuts.

Lemon, Honey and Vanilla Mousse with Blackberry Compote

SERVES 4

Blackberry compote

1½ cups fresh or frozen blackberries

2 tbsp honey

2–3 tbsp water

Mousse

2 cups cream or coconut cream

2 tsp gelatin (I buy one that's made from grass-fed animals)

2 tsp pure vanilla extract

¼ cup honey

juice of 1 lemon

Blackberries have me imagining all kinds of painterly desserts of the 'dark and moody' theme. I just love their deep tartness and romantic purple hue. Here, soft and sumptuous blackberry compote is layered with a pure, creamy-coloured mousse. This recipe calls for honey to sweeten, and a touch of vanilla — just enough to enhance the dessert, without being overpowering. Serve in small portions and devour with a teaspoon.

To make the compote, put all the ingredients in a small saucepan over medium heat. Bring to a soft boil and then lower the heat and simmer for 5 minutes or so, until the berries release their juices and become tender. Set aside to cool while you prepare the mousse.

Pour the cream into a medium-sized saucepan, sprinkle over the gelatin, and allow to bloom for 5 minutes.

Heat on low while stirring continuously until the gelatin has fully dissolved. Add the vanilla, honey and lemon juice and cook until gently steaming and a few bubbles rise around the edges of the pot, taking care not to let it boil.

Remove from the heat and allow to cool for a few minutes.

Pour the mixture into a container with a lid and place in the fridge to set for at least 6 hours or overnight.

To assemble, layer the compote and mousse in 4 small glasses or jars, finishing with a layer of compote.

Serve chilled.

Nurture Friendships

———

Over the years, I've learnt how easy it is to lose touch with old friends. Although we might think about them from time to time, or follow their lives in the online world, the act of reaching out can so easily be forgotten.

Close friendships are important on so many levels and when we truly and authentically invest in our friendships, we can create the kind of bond that's deeply precious. Our closest friends are our rocks: they often know everything about us and have the ability to love despite our shortcomings and quirks, they know what makes us feel good and ultimately, are the ones who are there when we need support.

And so, even when life gets busy, I make an effort to reach out to those I love the most. This might be a simple phone call to see how they are, or a quick message to let them know I am thinking of them. The best catch-up, in my mind, is over a cup of tea and something sweet to nibble on. A nature walk together is a lovely idea, too.

Date Night at Home

———

It can be difficult to create romance with your significant other amidst busy lives, especially if you have small children. My husband and I often create a date night within the walls of our little home. I love the idea of creating a delicious, home-cooked meal — something a little special to enjoy together.

Polenta and Almond Crumbed Fish

SERVES 2

handful of parsley, finely chopped

¾ cup almond meal

½ cup polenta

1 tsp sea salt

2 free-range eggs

400g white fish fillets

butter for cooking

Imagine a simple dinner of fish — crisp and lemony on the outside, and succulent through the middle — served with a salad of lettuce and herbs picked straight from the garden, tossed gently with lemon juice and a heavy drizzle of buttery olive oil. This meal could be the basis for a magical evening for two.

In a large, shallow bowl, combine the parsley, almond meal, polenta and sea salt.

Crack the eggs into a separate bowl and beat lightly.

Dip each piece of fish into the egg, then coat in the almond meal mixture.

Place a large skillet or pan over medium heat. Add 1–2 tablespoons of butter and swirl to coat the base. Cook the fish for 2–3 minutes on each side or until golden and crispy and cooked through.

Serve with a herby green salad, some lemon halves and some tomato relish or perhaps a dollop of Greek yoghurt.

Grow Your Own

———

The sweet, fresh scent of a vegetable garden in full bloom is warm, fragrant and inspiring. It's a sanctuary to escape to, immerse our hands in the warm soil, and connect with nature in a way like no other.

Growing your own vegetables and eating seasonally is one of the simplest ways to tread lightly on this earth. Whether you're new to gardening or a seasoned expert, there are things to be learnt with each plant you grow.

If you don't have space for a big plot in your backyard, you could try growing your own salad greens and herbs in container gardens, a few small clay pots on your windowsill, or a little wooden planter box outside your doorstep. Many neighbourhoods have community gardens, too. It can be a lovely way to meet new faces and learn some new tips.

Whenever I'm feeling at a loss as to what to cook for dinner, I'll walk around the garden, looking for inspiration. Letting my senses guide me, I'll fill a bowl with a few fresh ingredients, and conjure up something nourishing to eat.

Herbed Lentil Salad with Salmon and Preserved Lemon

SERVES 4 AS A SIDE OR 2 AS A MAIN

400g can lentils

1 large shallot, finely sliced

2 large handfuls basil, roughly chopped

2 tbsp finely sliced preserved lemon

100g smoked salmon, torn into pieces

1½ cups cherry tomatoes, quartered

¼ cup capers, drained

¼ cup extra virgin olive oil

¼ cup apple cider vinegar

I make variations of this punchy, bright salad on a weekly basis, as it's ridiculously easy and healthy. It can easily be adapted depending on what you have on hand or growing in your garden — cucumber or ribbons of carrot can replace the cherry tomatoes, or perhaps you've got some baby spinach or rocket to toss through. When I've got a little more time up my sleeve, I'll add slices of grilled eggplant or courgette. This salad can be made in advance, and will keep overnight in the fridge. If making in advance, toss through the olive oil and vinegar just before serving.

Combine all ingredients in a large bowl or serving platter.

Toss well and season with flaky salt and freshly ground black pepper to taste.

Finding Your Quiet Place

———

Whenever I'm feeling overwhelmed, I head down to the bay that is a fifteen-minute walk from our home. With its small, sandy beach and shallow, glistening water, there's something about this place that evokes calmness and gently reminds me to slow down. In summer there are blossoming pohutukawa trees, with leaves turning silver in the sun. There is birdsong overhead and gentle, shimmering waves. It's here in this open space that I am able to take refuge when needing a change of perspective or simply a moment of quiet.

I've needed quite a few of these moments recently while writing this book and caring for my little ones at home, because motherhood, despite all its beauty, can be hard. So I come to the beach by myself, and spread out a blanket to sit on. I can take off my sandals and feel the sand between my toes; it's a place to embrace the richly tangible. This is my quiet place — I hope you can find yours.

The Magic of Music

———————

Music can influence us on so many levels. Whether it be soothing, enlivening or uplifting, music touches your soul and deeply affects your mood.

Perhaps we should be treating music the same way we do exercise and wholesome food, aiming to incorporate it into our daily lives. Maybe we should acknowledge that music can be an essential part of our wellbeing, too.

Next time you're feeling a little off balance, turn on some music. Whether it be gentle, instrumental or spiritual, close your eyes and take a moment to allow it to permeate deep within your being. Let it flow into you, and out of you — narrating a calm and steady rhythm of the kind of life you want to live.

Celebrate
Your Belongings

———————

Once you've cleared the clutter from your home, you might begin to notice your nicest things more and feel naturally inclined to use them on a daily basis, rather than saving them for a special occasion that might never come. There's no reason why you shouldn't use your best china when you eat your lunch, or feel frivolous if you allow your children to use linen napkins instead of paper towels. It might even begin to feel like a good idea to slip on that lovely silk dress when you pop down to the local shops. There's so much pleasure to be had in enjoying our most loved items on a daily basis. After all, we deserve to use the best we have.

Beautiful Blooms

Simply looking at flowers, with their intricate detail and beautiful hues, instantly improves my mood and puts a smile on my face. It's for this reason that I like to keep a vase of flowers on my kitchen windowsill, as well as a few smaller arrangements around the house in unexpected places, such as the children's rooms and the bathroom. These little whispers of nature might be small touches, but they brighten up any space tremendously.

We've learned to ask where our food comes from, and how our clothes are manufactured, but what about that bouquet of flowers? Some might not realise that the blooms we buy from the supermarket, or sometimes the local florist, have been flown halfway around the world, and are commonly sprayed with chemicals to keep them fresh.

Thankfully, the appeal of locally grown, seasonal flowers is beginning to catch on. You can also plant your own, seek out local growers, or forage for wild flowers.

Forage and Find

———

Most of the blooms that I bring into our home have been gathered from our own garden or from neighbourhood walks or park rambles. In addition to roadside wildflowers, if you have bush nearby, our natural environment also offers an abundance of ferns and foliage that look lovely in arrangements.

That's the beauty of foraging — it opens your eyes to all the wild and romantic things growing around you, and once you start looking, you'll suddenly notice flora you wouldn't have noticed before. The more I look, the more I become familiar with the abundance of seasonal beauty, right there, just begging to be welcomed into our home.

If you are going to forage for flora and foliage, it's important to be respectful of other people's property and of mother nature. Only take what you need, leaving some for the next person to enjoy.

A Seasonal Guide to Flowers

───────────

Spring

bougainvillea
cherry blossom
cornflower
daffodil
freesia
gardenia
iris
jasmine
lavender
lilac
magnolia
peony
poppy
wisteria

Summer

Angelica
blackberry
cosmos
dahlia
fennel flower
foxglove
hydrangea
Indian mallow
Queen Anne's
 lace
rosehip
sunflower
thistle
tiger lily
waterlily

Autumn

allium
amaranth
anemone
chrysanthemum
crab apple
 blossom
protea
ranunculus
snowberry

Winter

calendula
camellia
eucalyptus
hellebore
kale flower
lichen
orchid
pansy
snap dragon
tulip
wild rose
winter lily

A Romantic Flower Arrangement

When it comes to styling a dreamy vase of flowers, I like to bring it back to basics and keep them as simple as possible. One way to do this is to use a balance of three components. One or two blooms, one leafy green, and one textural or unexpected element.

Once you've chosen the stems you'd like to use, give each a fresh cut on an angle, but keep a good length — you can always trim them again later if you need to.

Begin by placing a few of the larger textural elements around the edge of the vase, allowing them to spill over the edges. Next distribute any leafy greens in and around the arrangement, followed by the floral stems, filling any gaps as you go.

Stand back a little and admire your arrangement from a few different angles; you can make small changes if you need to, or trim certain stems if necessary. Remember, it doesn't need to be perfectly formed — a feeling of wildness and movement can add texture and interest.

explore

One of the greatest forms of medicine is one that surrounds us. The effect nature can have on our soul is deep, magical and captivating. It's something so simple, yet more often than not, we rarely take enough time to appreciate our surroundings, and the strength it has to offer us.

Whenever I'm feeling off balance, I step into nature. The soft hues of green and blue soothe my mind with a sense of clarity and perspective. When I stare out into the ocean, I feel humbled. I am reminded to embrace things that bring me joy, and to let go of those that do not. The wind seems to disperse my worries, each one disappearing into the big, beautiful landscape.

Next time you're feeling overwhelmed by the burdens of day-to-day life, I hope that you can escape into nature. You'll be glad that you did, and those around you will be glad, too.

Move Your Body

———

Do you sometimes feel that you are just going through the motions instead of fully living? I used to live this way, always waiting for the next big thing to happen, and it felt as if life was passing me by. It wasn't until I started going for slow daily walks that I began to really notice the world around me and appreciate life for what it is. With each step it was as if I could *physically feel* a weight lifting — the fog would clear from my mind with each slow, deep breath.

I now make the time to step outside and go for a walk most days. I let my mind wander along with my body, noticing the small pieces of life I come across. It's something I love to do in solitude, but it can also be a wonderful experience with your children, too. It's a daily ritual that I always look forward to, and I hope you will, too.

Farmers' Markets

———————

I like to be mindful of where our food comes from, whether it be beetroot from the garden or a jar of local honey from the farmers' markets. Knowing where the ingredients originated helps me to connect with the story behind what I choose to feed my family. Not only has this helped me to create a great relationship with food, I have also gained a deeper appreciation for each and every thing I create in the kitchen.

It's not surprising that our shopping habits have changed quite considerably over the years. Most weekends my family enjoys visiting our local markets — it's become a lovely family ritual that revives the soul and inspires meals for the week ahead. It's so lovely to be able to meet the growers and artisans who produce the food we eat; I love striking up conversations with them and hearing their passion for the products they create.

Quite often you'll find unique items beyond produce, such as meat and eggs, locally fermented kombucha, organic dog treats, or heritage seeds and seedlings. We love to try out new stands each week, and be a little adventurous with our choices.

The growing popularity of farmers' markets is seen worldwide, which is great, because eating locally and seasonally is good for you, the environment and your community. So go ahead and scout out the closest farmers' market to you. Just be sure to take along your reusable shopping bag to fill with goodies.

Explore Your Own Neighbourhood

Whether you've lived in your neighbourhood for years or have recently made the move, I'm sure there will be plenty of new, exciting places close by that you've never noticed before. Your home town can be a new source of adventure and inspiration, it's simply up to you to explore it.

First, spend some time studying a map of your area; you might be surprised at what you can find close to home. You might like to explore by foot, or perhaps by bicycle. Investigate whether there are any free outdoor events or concerts taking place by checking your local newspaper. You might even be interested in helping out as a volunteer. Wander around the local shops, or pop into a café or restaurant you haven't visited before, and don't be afraid to introduce yourself to new people you meet along the way.

Write a list of any local bush walks, coastal tracks or parks you'd like to explore. Pack a picnic, escape for the day, and soak up some beautiful scenery.

Day Trip

———

Close to home, there's a sleepy seaside village that we visit often. We wander along the gentle trickling creek, and up past the battered old skate ramp. I find a little shade under a big old tree next to the ocean, the fresh scent of salt and sea perfectly complementing the rhythm of the waves. We eat together, passing plates, pouring iced tea. There is garlicky butter bean dip with sourdough and crisp vegetables for dipping and little Black Doris plum pies with buttery yoghurt pastry. And in that moment, I begin to feel the tenseness in my muscles loosen, my racing mind slow and the rhythm of my breath soften. We begin to feel full, not only from the nourishment of food, but from the enjoyment of gathering together.

Roasted Garlic and Butter Bean Hummus

MAKES ABOUT 2 CUPS

1 bulb garlic, sliced in half horizontally

extra virgin olive oil for drizzling

400g can butter beans, drained

handful fresh Italian parsley

¼ cup extra virgin olive oil

juice of 1 large lemon

To serve

toasted sesame seeds

A dip of velvety butter beans and pungent roasted garlic. It's delicious spread on toast, too, with a few slices of tomato and freshly ground pepper.

Preheat the oven to 180°C.

Place the garlic in a small roasting dish, flesh side up. Drizzle with extra virgin olive oil and roast until tender, about 20 minutes.

Allow to cool, then squeeze the flesh out of the papery skins and put into the bowl of a food processor along with the remaining ingredients. Process until smooth, or to your liking. Season with flaky sea salt and freshly ground pepper to taste.

Serve with crackers, sourdough bread or raw vegetable sticks for dipping. Sprinkle with toasted sesame seeds to serve.

Black Doris Plum and Boysenberry Pies with Yoghurt Spelt Pastry

MAKES 18 MINI PIES

Fruit filling

1 cup boysenberries

6 Black Doris plums, de-stoned and roughly chopped

4 tbsp honey or pure maple syrup

1 tsp pure vanilla bean paste

juice of ½ lemon

Pastry

200g chilled unsalted butter, diced

2 cups wholemeal spelt flour, plus extra for kneading

½ cup coconut, rapadura or light muscovado sugar

½ cup natural Greek yoghurt

pinch of sea salt

To finish

¼ cup milk for brushing

cinnamon for sprinkling

My children just love these sweet little hand pies. The plum, boysenberry and honey filling is encased in a yoghurt and spelt flour pastry, which is perfectly buttery with a crisp golden texture. A light dusting of cinnamon brings a soft warmness to the sweet fruit filling.

_____

Put the boysenberries, plums, honey and vanilla bean paste in a saucepan and cover with water. Cook over a medium heat until bubbling, then reduce the heat and simmer until soft, tender and syrupy — about 25 minutes. Add the lemon juice, and stir to combine.

To make the pastry, put the butter, flour and sugar in the bowl of a food processor and pulse until the mixture resembles breadcrumbs.

Add the yoghurt and salt, then continue to pulse until the dough begins to come together into a ball. Place the dough in the fridge to rest for 10–15 minutes.

Preheat the oven to 180°C and line two large baking trays with baking paper.

Roll the dough out on a lightly floured surface to about 5mm thick. Using a round cookie cutter (or the rim of a wide-mouthed cup or glass), cut out as many circles as you can.

CONTINUED ON NEXT PAGE

Black Doris Plum and Boysenberry Pies with Yoghurt Spelt Pastry

CONTINUED

Transfer half the dough rounds to the prepared trays, leaving 2cm between each. On each one, place about a tablespoon of the fruit filling in the middle of the circle, leaving a 1cm border of pastry around the edges.

Working with one round at a time, brush the edges with a little milk and pop a second circle on top. Use a fork to gently seal the edges. Repeat with the remaining dough circles.

Pierce each pie with a fork, then brush the tops with milk and sprinkle with cinnamon.

Bake for 20–25 minutes or until golden.

Remove from the oven and allow the pies to cool. They can be stored in an airtight container for up to 3 days.

share

Sharing food with those I love is what drives my passion for cooking. My idea of the perfect evening is to spend it with family and friends, the kind of get-together where hours pass fleetingly and conversation flows effortlessly. A natural kind of entertaining — relaxed, intentional and thoughtful. Over the next few pages I share my ideas for a simple yet elegant approach to entertaining family and friends, and how unique, unconventional settings can often leave us with far more intriguing memories.

Setting the Table

———

To set the table nicely is to announce a change of mood, to suggest we savour the meal with utmost care and appreciate the pleasure of sharing food with those we love.

There doesn't have to be fancy crockery, crystal glasses or expensive serveware. I believe that by keeping it simple and working with nature's elements you can create a warm, inviting table that engages the senses with seasonal beauty.

For example, an apple-tree branch makes an interesting centrepiece, complete with its organically beautiful fruit. Or perhaps create a garland made out of dried leaves, showcasing an autumn-themed palette of orange, red and dusty brown. If your guests are visiting in wintertime, you might like to place small jars filled with fragrant herbs such as sage, rosemary or oregano around the table.

Keep to a simple palette of colours, and introduce a little texture in the way of linen, placemats or perhaps a table runner. I prefer to leave the flowers or foliage until last, adding a final flourish to the table.

A Little Charm

———

Beautiful little details can add charm and uniqueness to even the smallest of occasions. Whether it's handwritten place cards, a sprig of eucalyptus on each place setting, or inspiring quotes popped into an envelope for each guest, these are the things that will leave a lasting impression and add character to your table.

Luscious wild foliage is a lovely way to get inspired by the seasons and use what you might find in your back garden or at the local farmers' market. I love to arrange flowers and foliage among the serveware, or place a large vase at the end of the table, filled haphazardly with blossoms tumbling over the side. Whole pieces of fruit such as fig, pear or apple can also look visually stunning, and can add a certain earthy aesthetic.

Embrace Napkins

You might think of napkins as an old-fashioned choice, others might say they are pointless, but how do you wipe your fingers? And what do you use to dab your chin when devouring delectable, buttery asparagus? A lifeless paper towel just isn't the same, really. Once you fall into the habit of using napkins, you might even find you simply can't dine without them. I personally love linen for its lasting quality and the softness that comes with each wash. They also act as a lovely place setting for your guest, rolled simply and topped with a sprig of rosemary, or perhaps tied with a piece of twine.

Ambient Lighting

———

In a world of artificial lighting, I much prefer the natural kind. Imagine an early evening picnic surrounding a bonfire, or a cosy dinner accented with the flicker of candlelight.

Candles shouldn't compete with the fragrance of what you're serving for dinner, so it's best to use pure, unscented beeswax or soy candles as part of your setting.

A Simple Seasonal Menu

When it comes to the menu, I prefer to keep it simple with basic, seasonal dishes. I almost always prepare most of the food a few hours beforehand, and simply add any finishing touches before serving. What's the point of having guests over for dinner if you are tucked away in the kitchen the entire evening?

Roast Chicken with White Wine, Basil and Tomato

SERVES 3–4

1kg free-range chicken thighs or drumsticks

6 cloves garlic, crushed using the back of a heavy knife

1 lemon, quartered

1 punnet cherry tomatoes, sliced in half

100ml white wine

extra virgin olive oil for drizzling

handful of fresh basil

This is the kind of meal that can restore your love for life. Sumptuously sweet and salty chicken, slow roasted in a sauce of white wine, garlic, lemon, basil and tomatoes. There's also soft and succulent butter beans mingling among all the gorgeous flavours.

Preheat the oven to 180°C.

Arrange the chicken, garlic, lemon and tomatoes in a large roasting dish. Pour the white wine over the top, drizzle generously with extra virgin olive oil, and scatter the basil over the top. Season with flaky sea salt and freshly ground black pepper.

Bake in the oven for 1 hour or until golden and succulent and the juices run clear.

Remove from the oven and leave to cool slightly before serving.

Simple Salad Greens, Well Dressed

SERVES 4 AS A SIDE

Buttermilk dressing

½ cup buttermilk or natural yoghurt

¼ cup extra virgin olive oil

small handful of fresh dill, basil and parsley, finely sliced

juice of 1 lemon

1 tbsp Dijon mustard

1 shallot, finely sliced

Salad

4 large handfuls of endive lettuce or lettuce of your choice

1 cup slivered almonds, lightly toasted

50g Pecorino cheese, shaved into long slithers

½ cucumber, sliced in half lengthways and then quartered and thinly sliced (optional)

There is so much pleasure to be had in simple salad greens, dressed perfectly. Curly endive is the star of this dish with its crisp leaves and slightly bitter flavour. Lightly tossed in tangy buttermilk vinaigrette, this recipe is simple but elegant.

Combine dressing ingredients in a small bowl. Whisk until creamy, and then season with salt and freshly ground black pepper to taste.

Gently rinse the lettuce in cold water, discarding any tough outer leaves. Soak the washed leaves in iced water for 10 minutes. This helps the leaves to become extra crisp. Drain and dry the leaves, and arrange on a serving platter along with the almonds, pecorino cheese and cucumber (if using).

Serve the salad with a generous drizzle of the dressing.

Braised Eggplant with Fragrant Herbs

SERVES 4 AS A SIDE

glug of extra virgin olive oil

2 eggplants, cubed

1 large fennel bulb, finely sliced*

2 cups vegetable or chicken stock

2 tbsp white balsamic vinegar

¼ cup capers, drained

handful of mint, roughly chopped

handful of basil, roughly chopped

handful of Italian flat leaf parsley, roughly chopped

A quite wonderful recipe, this — unfussy to make, and to eat. Simply place the ingredients into a large pot and allow the heat to do the rest. This dish is lovely served with grilled fish or chicken, tossed through pasta or spooned over buttery mash.

———————————

Place a heavy-bottomed cast-iron pot over a medium heat. Add enough olive oil to cover the bottom entirely.

Once oil is sizzling, add the eggplant and fennel and stir to coat in the oil. Add the stock, cover the pot, then reduce the heat down as low as you can.

Cook for 25–30 minutes or until tender. The eggplant should be meltingly soft. You might need to add a splash of water or two if it starts to stick on the bottom.

Remove from the heat, add the white balsamic vinegar, capers, herbs (reserving some for garnish) and a generous pinch of sea salt and freshly ground black pepper. Stir until combined.

Serve warm with a sprinkle of fresh herbs.

*If you can't find fennel, leek or shallots would also work well here.

Pistachio Cake with Lemon Curd

MAKES ONE 23CM CAKE

Cake

3 large lemons

1 cup pistachios

1 cup ground almonds

¼ cup honey

½ cup coconut, rapadura
or light muscovado sugar

5 free-range eggs

1 tsp vanilla extract

1 tsp baking soda

Lemon curd

⅓ cup melted coconut oil
or unsalted butter

¼ cup honey

2 tsp pure vanilla extract

4 free-range eggs

½ cup lemon juice

To decorate

½ cup mascarpone

1 cup fresh blueberries

½ cup crushed pistachios

This deeply moist and soft cake is scented with pistachios
and sweetened with honey. A nutty cake needs something
to offset its deepness, and a smothering of mascarpone
and lemon curd does the trick quite nicely.

Place the whole lemons in a large saucepan and cover with
water. Bring to the boil and then lower heat and simmer
for 1 hour. Drain and then allow to cool.

Preheat the oven to 160°C and grease a 23cm cake tin
with butter or coconut oil.

Cut the lemons in half, remove and discard the pips, and
place lemons into the bowl of a food processor (skin, pith,
flesh and all). Process until smooth. Add the remaining
cake ingredients and process again until smooth.

Pour the batter into the prepared cake tin and use a
spatula to smooth out evenly. Bake for 35–40 minutes
or until a skewer inserted in the middle comes out clean.
Leave to cool in the tin.

To make the lemon curd, put the coconut oil or butter,
honey and vanilla into a small saucepan and melt together
over a medium heat. Remove from the heat and allow to
cool for a minute or so. Once cooled, carefully whisk in
the eggs and lemon juice.

CONTINUED ON NEXT PAGE

Pistachio Cake with Lemon Curd

Place back over a low heat, then continue to whisk for 2–3 minutes or until the curd becomes lovely and thick. Remove from the heat. Leave to cool before using.

Once the cake has cooled completely, carefully transfer to a plate.

Put the lemon curd and mascarpone in a bowl, and mix until smooth.

Top the cake with the lemon curd mascarpone icing, fresh blueberries, and a sprinkle of crushed pistachios.

Will keep for 2–3 days in an airtight container.

The Perfect Cheese Platter

Beautiful, pungent and rich, there's something about cheese that I simply can't resist. It's not surprising that I have a deep love for creating the perfect cheese board, one with varying textures, colours and flavours. Not only are tasting platters relatively simple to throw together, they can also be a conversation piece for your guests. Most will dig in with gusto, sharing opinions about which cheese they like, and perhaps those they don't.

Here are some simple tips to help you create the perfect cheese platter.

Choose a large platter that will fit a good selection of ingredients. I often use a round wooden chopping board with a piece of baking paper placed on top.

I like to keep it minimal and offer three different types of cheese of varying textures and age — you don't want to overwhelm anyone's palate. The first is a soft, creamy cheese such as Brie or Camembert. Mild, whipped ricotta would also work nicely here. The second is something firm and aged, such as a sharp vintage Cheddar, Gruyère, or Gouda. The third is blue vein, my most loved variety; almost every cheese board I make includes a blue cheese, known for its intensely strong and pungent aroma. I also recommend trying out cheeses made with different types of milk, such as goat or sheep milk.

Dry cheese often likes something creamy to accompany it, such as slices of avocado, whereas salty cheese begs for something sweet, such as thin slices of fresh pear or apple. Fresh berries are another thought. Decorate with honeycomb and a few sprigs of rosemary to create a platter that's visually striking — remember that people often eat with their eyes first.

Always offer a different knife with each cheese variety. If guests help themselves to the cheese using just one knife, there is a high chance that all the cheeses might start tasting like one another.

Various other sweet and salty items work well as an accompaniment to cheese. Try cured goods such as prosciutto, salami or smoked salmon, salty morsels such as pistachios, candied almonds or good-quality olives. Assorted dried fruit can include figs, medjool dates, prunes or apricots.

Forget flavoured crackers and try something a little more interesting. I enjoy oat crackers for their mild, buttery flavour but good-quality sourdough or French baguette are also nice options, particularly if you include a little bowl of extra virgin olive oil for dipping.

Always bring your cheese to room temperature before serving — cheese at room temperature reveals flavour subtleties that you don't taste if it's chilled. I like to pop it on the table at least an hour before guests arrive.

Lastly, I recommend making as many selections as you can from local producers. I like to visit my local farmers' market or, alternatively, a local delicatessen will offer a beautiful variety of cheese and is always happy to help out.

The 'other' press machine

She said she'd have a word with the editor about our scheme as
she thought it would be 'right up her alley'. We waited a polite
number of days before following anything up—a casual e-mail asking about the children, the husband, before dropping in a throw-
away question about whether she'd had a chance to mention anything about us to the editor of ... now what was it ... the Telegraph?
Oh no, that Observer supplement, whatever it's called, wasn't it?
The expectant wait for a reply was soon rewarded with a long e-
mail detailing the extra-curricular exploits of the various children,
and then at the end so ... Oh yes, I did mention it. She is really
on you ...

rest

———

Sleep is a wonderful thing. We spend a third of our lives doing it, and it's essential for the healing of our bodies, so why is it that many of us have trouble sleeping?

More often than not, we zoom through the day at lightning speed, our minds running wild with to-do lists and the busyness of daily life. It's no wonder we find it hard to slip into a deep and peaceful slumber.

Over the past few years, I've learnt to embrace the slow, methodical pace of an evening routine. Not only do these small, simple rituals help me to unwind, I consider them to be magical little moments — just for me, and nobody else.

In this chapter, I've shared a few ideas to help you unwind, as well as a handful of my favourite night-time recipes including spiced apple cider and creamy chamomile and honey nut milk tea.

Whatever rituals work for you, practice them habitually. Your mind and body will naturally embrace the rhythm, and instinctively know it's time to slow down.

Light a Candle

———

As night falls each evening, I wander around the house lighting a series of candles. It's a beautiful reminder to prepare my body for rest, and to watch as the evening slowly unfolds.

Even my children have come to know that as soon as the candles are flickering gently in the dim light, it's time to relax and prepare for bed.

Not only do candles create lovely ambience, dim lighting can stimulate melatonin in our bodies, which helps us to connect to our circadian rhythms.

It might seem like a rather simple ritual, but it's too simple not to try, don't you think?

Evening Rhythms for Little Ones

———

Truth be told, there are evenings when getting the kids to bed can seem quite the chore. I can feel weary by nightfall and find my patience waning. Over the years I have found that establishing a bedtime routine is essential for creating a soothing evening rhythm, not only for our little ones but for us as parents, too.

———

If you've got little ones, I'm sure you're familiar with the dreadful witching hour (or two) that comes before bedtime. It's a time when we all feel tired and easily frustrated. We've found that the best thing to do is to go for a gentle walk. These walks are the most beautiful way to unwind after a long day and prepare for a slow, restful evening, and we often head out just before dinner.

It goes without saying that a nice, hot bath is one of the most comforting ways to relax. Let your little ones choose an essential oil and then add a few drops to the water along with a little coconut oil or almond oil for soft, silky skin.

Once they hop out of the bath, allow them to get dressed into sleepwear themselves, and pick out the next morning's outfit. My little ones love having this choice, and I find it makes the bedtime routine a little more enjoyable for both of us.

Spray some homemade pillow spray (page 210) on their pillows and blankets before tucking them in. Not only does this create a calming environment, it smells gorgeous, too.

Snuggle in with them, and read a book. Avoid the 'one more please' pattern by establishing beforehand how many books you'll read.

Pop on some soft, soothing music, turn the lights down low, and talk quietly about their day. If your little ones are feeling wound up, it's the perfect time to release any worries and connect in a way that's meaningful. Another idea is to ask them to 'pick a dream', allowing them to drift off with warm, fuzzy thoughts.

Last but not least, the key to a good bedtime routine is to pick a specific time and stick with it! Their little body clocks will adapt, and fall into a natural rhythm.

Something Slow

———————

Distractions can be exhausting. Whether it's your phone lighting up constantly or the flashing television in the background, it's these distractions that unapologetically demand our attention — if we allow them to.

Do you take time to slow down each evening and savour life at a slower pace? When was the last time you simply said 'stop' to the world around you and reignited your passion for things that authentically bring you joy?

Spending a few hours cooking something delicious in the kitchen, getting lost in a romance novel, or simply hanging out in the lounge with my husband are things that help me slow down. Sometimes we pull out a board game, or play a round of cards. On a fine evening, we might snuggle up outside with a blanket and a hot drink while gazing at the stars and enjoying quiet conversation.

I hope that you too will make time in the evening to enjoy moments that bring you joy and comfort. Find what works for you, and turn it into a night-time ritual.

A Bathing Ritual

———————

Most evenings I indulge in a long, hot bath. It's a simple pleasure that does wonders for the soul and helps me to relax. Imagine the soft flicker of candles burning, rocks of pink salt dissolving into the steaming water to help with muscle relaxation, and the soul-soothing aroma of essential oils diffusing into the air. Sometimes I'll add a handful of fresh petals to the bath water for a rejuvenating floral soak.

The bath is my oasis, a magical place to take much-needed time out from the world and my responsibilities. It's a place to clear my mind and find that beautiful thing we call balance.

Once I have slipped into a sweet state of relaxation, I often welcome an intention into my mind and spend a few moments focusing on its manifestation. It might be an area of my life that needs to change, or perhaps something I'm working towards and would like to see blossom.

Over the next few pages, you'll find a couple of bath soak recipes using simple, natural ingredients. I make these often, and I hope you will enjoy them, too.

Oatmeal and Lavender Bath Soak

MAKES 2 BAGS

1 cup rolled oats

½ cup dried lavender flowers

2 small rounds of muslin cloth or cotton drawstring bags

cotton ribbon or twine

Nothing induces relaxation quite like the scent of lavender, and particularly so in this milky bath soak. Oatmeal has soothing qualities and can help to soften, calm and nourish dry or itchy skin. You might as well make a few, as these little parcels also make a lovely gift.

Put the rolled oats into the bowl of a food processor and pulse until a fine meal forms.

Put the ground oats and lavender flowers in a small bowl and toss until combined.

Spoon the oat mixture between the rounds of cloth, then one at a time, bring up the corners to make a little bag. Tie tightly with ribbon or twine.

To use, simply put a bag into a warm bath. Once softened, squeeze the bag to get the milky liquid out of the oats. You can also use the bag to gently exfoliate your skin.

Coconut Milk, Vanilla and Pink Salt Bath Soak

MAKES 2–2½ CUPS

1 cup pink Himalayan rock salts

1 cup coconut milk powder*

10 drops vanilla essential oil

½ cup dried rose petals (optional)

Perfect for hydrating and softening the skin, this coconut milk, vanilla and rose bath soak is luxuriously indulgent and will leave you smelling lovely. Pink Himalayan salt infuses your bathing water with minerals and helps with relaxation.

———————————

Put all the ingredients into a bowl and toss gently to combine. Transfer to a dark-coloured glass jar to store.

Keep the jar in a cool, dark place, and use within a month or two.

To use, add a large handful to your bath and allow it to dissolve in the hot water. It's best to do this right before you hop in the bath as this is when the essential oils are most fragrant. Inhale deeply and enjoy.

*You could also use cow's milk or almond milk powder.

Write It Down

———

Racing and irrational thoughts and trivial unresolved worries can keep us awake. I like to keep a journal or diary on my bedside table and write down any to-dos or things that seem to be swimming around in my mind before bed.

I also take this opportunity to take note of the things I'm grateful for; a cosy bed to sleep in, the delicious dinner we enjoyed earlier, the roof over our heads. Practising gratitude sends a warm feeling through my bones, and inspires a lovely sense of contentment — just what is needed when falling into bed.

Indulge in
Beautiful Sleepwear

Finding beauty in every day can be as simple as luxu-
riating in lovely sleepwear. We spend many hours of our
day sleeping, and yet, most of us don't give much thought
to what we wear to bed. I have to admit, I seem to fall
into a more restful sleep when I'm wearing something that
makes me feel pretty.

Thankfully, there are plenty of emerging sleepwear
designers that offer natural fibres such as linen, silk and
organic cotton. In summer, I love pure cotton for its
lightweight feel, breathability and texture that softens
with each wash. And during winter, cosy sleepwear made
out of merino wool or cashmere is sensuously soft on the
skin and exquisite to wear.

Whatever your preference might be, I believe we all
deserve a little bedtime luxury.

Making a Cosy Bed

I believe that to have a good night's sleep you need to feel cosy and comfortable in bed. To slumber in soft, clean linen is one of life's simple pleasures, and one that we can enjoy each and every night.

There is something to be said for bedding that has spent time in the sunshine, and the clean smell of freshly dried linen can't be beaten. Homemade natural washing powder (see recipe on page 90) works wonders, too.

I appreciate good-quality linen, not only for its softness, but because I know it will last for years to come. I also enjoy having plenty of pillows on the bed, and like to surround myself with them while sleeping to feel extra cosy. Flowers or greenery by the bedside adds a beautiful touch, too.

Whatever your taste, make sure you arrange your bed exactly how you like it, and you'll wake the next morning ready to embrace the beautiful new day waiting for you.

Chamomile and Lemon Pillow Spray

MAKES 250ML

40ml witch hazel

200ml distilled water

10 drops chamomile essential oil

5 drops lemon essential oil

This blend of chamomile and lemon essential oils is both refreshing and soothing. Mist it onto your body as a light fragrance or spray it onto your pillow for a restful sleep. Lavender and rose essential oils also make for a lovely, calming combination.

Pour all the ingredients into a small dark-coloured spray bottle.

Shake gently to combine before using.

Warm Apple Cider with Spices

SERVES 2

2 cups water

4 tbsp apple cider vinegar

2 tbsp honey

2 cinnamon quills

¼ tsp nutmeg

¼ tsp ground ginger

peel of 1 orange

3–4 star anise

This is a warm, golden drink for a cold winter's evening. Orange peel, star anise, cinnamon and honey combine in a warming glass of goodness. You'll be delighted to find it fills the home with a beautiful aroma, too.

———————

Combine all ingredients in a small saucepan over medium heat. Bring to a gentle simmer, stirring continuously, and then set aside to cool slightly.

Pour into glasses or mugs and enjoy.

Hot Cacao Elixir

SERVES 2

2 cups nut milk (I like to use almond, cashew or hazelnut)

2 tbsp cacao powder

1 tsp maca powder (optional)

1 tsp pure vanilla extract

½ tsp cinnamon

tiny pinch of sea salt

2 tbsp pure maple syrup

This happiness-inducing recipe should do the trick on those nights when you crave a little chocolate. Cacao is exceptionally good for you, and when married with velvety nut milk and a dash of pure maple syrup, it's even more spectacular.

Put all the ingredients into a saucepan over low heat. Stir occasionally until gently steaming.

Pour into mugs and enjoy.

Creamy Chamomile, Honey and Nut Milk Tea

SERVES 2

2 cups nut milk

2 chamomile tea bags

1 tsp pure vanilla extract

1 tbsp honey

The infusion of chamomile in this creamy, hot tea helps me to feel ready for a good night's sleep. It's lightly sweetened with a little honey, although pure maple syrup works well, too. The creaminess comes from steeping the tea in nut milk. I know this might seem a little unusual, but it's surprisingly delicious.

Put all the ingredients into a small saucepan over medium heat. Bring to a gentle simmer, stirring continuously, and then set aside to cool slightly.

Remove the tea bags, pour into mugs and enjoy.

When you live a life that's less complicated, the world seems to have a beautiful way of opening up opportunities for you to find joy and meaning even in the most ordinary of things. I've found an entirely new way to live — one that's filled with balance, happiness and simplicity. This experience inspired me to put these thoughts onto paper to share with you. Perhaps you'll be inspired to pursue your own rhythms and routines, and maybe you will find a more fulfilling and enjoyable lifestyle, not only for you, but for your loved ones, too.

Recipe Index

Household Index

_____

Acknowledgements

A huge thank you to the fantastic team at Penguin Random House New Zealand, and in particular, to my wonderful publisher Debra. Thank you for having faith in me, and for your ongoing encouragement. It's a beautiful thing to see this book come to life just as I imagined it to be. To Tessa — your attention to detail is impeccable, thank you for making everything read so gracefully. To Rachel, your design encapsulates everything this book is about, and it's utterly wonderful, and Sarah, thank you for knitting it all together so nicely.

To my family and friends who helped out with the kids when I needed to sneak away to the library to write — you know who you are! Your kindness, generosity and ideas have helped to shape this book, and I couldn't have done it without you.

Thank you to Jonny, Bonnie and Ali from Tessuti for helping to put together the lovely dinner setting in the garden. The imagery and styling turned out just as romantic as I envisioned it to be. A special mention to Harman Grubisa for the pretty dress, too.

Thanks to Mavis and Osborn, Laing Home, George and Willy, and Bohome and Roam for your generosity and beautiful wares. I appreciate them greatly.

Much love and thanks to Dawn Clayden who made many of the gorgeous ceramics you will see pictured throughout these pages. Thank you Dawn, I will treasure them forever.

To my readers, whether you've joined me recently on this journey, or have been here from the start, I'd like to thank you for your kindness, honesty and interest in what I do. I am forever grateful, and look forward to many more conversations about all things simple (and delicious).

Last, but by no means least, thank you to my beautiful children, Bella, Obi and Archie, and my darling husband Valentin. You have been utterly patient, loving and supportive. Everything I do is for you.

Eleanor x

PENGUIN

UK | USA | Canada | Ireland | Australia
India | New Zealand | South Africa | China

Penguin is an imprint of the Penguin
Random House group of companies,
whose addresses can be found at
global.penguinrandomhouse.com.

Penguin
Random House
New Zealand

First published by
Penguin Random House New Zealand, 2017

10 9 8 7 6 5 4 3

Text and photography © Eleanor Ozich, 2017

The moral right of the author has been asserted.

Design by Rachel Clark
© Penguin Random House New Zealand
Author photograph and photographs
on pages 2, 32, 140, 162, 168, 172, 174–5,
177, 179, 181, 183, 218 and 222 by Jonny Scott
Prepress by Image Centre Group
Printed and bound in China by
RR Donnelley Asia

A catalogue record for this book is available
from the National Library of New Zealand.

ISBN 978-0-14-377123-4

penguin.co.nz

FSC
www.fsc.org

MIX
Paper from
responsible sources
FSC® C101537